PRAISE FO

'Beautifully c
imagination, this delightful collection
celebrates the natural world with tenderness,
wit and a true sense of wonder.'

Kate Wakeling, author of *Moon Juice*

'Vicky's knowledge and love of poetry and
nature have fizzed together to create something
wild and magical – a leaping, humming, shape-
shifting pack of forms of every kind. Each poem
glows with its own luminescence and invites us
to share in something amazing. *Aardvark Day* is
wonderful and wonder-full and I loved it.'

Rachel Piercey, editor of *Tyger Tyger Magazine*

OTHER TITLES AVAILABLE FROM THE EMMA PRESS

POETRY COLLECTIONS FOR CHILDREN
Poems from a Witch's Pocket, by Laura Theis, illus. by Kate Lucy Foster
Eggenwise, by Andrea Davidson, illus. by Amy Louise Evans
Balam and Lluvia's House, by Julio Serrano Echeverría, tr. from
Spanish by Lawrence Schimel, illus. by Yolanda Mosquera
Cloud Soup, by Kate Wakeling, illustrated by Elīna Brasliņa
My Sneezes Are Perfect, by Rakhshan Rizwan with Yusuf Samee,
illustrated by Benjamin Phillips

THEMED POETRY ANTHOLOGIES FOR CHILDREN
The Bee Is Not Afraid of Me: A Book of Insect Poems
Dragons of the Prime: Poems about Dinosaurs
The Head that Wears a Crown: Poems about Kings and Queens
Watcher of the Skies: Poems about Space and Aliens
Falling Out of the Sky: Poems about Myths and Monsters

CHAPTER BOOKS & SHORT STORIES FOR CHILDREN
Please Don't Read the Footnotes Please, by Rob Walton
The Skeleton in the Cupboard, and other stories, by Lilija Berzinska, tr.
from Latvian by Žanete Vēvere Pasqualini and Sara Smith
Na Willa and the House in the Alley, by Reda Gaudiamo, translated
from Indonesian by Ikhda Ayuning Maharsi Degoul and Kate
Wakeling, illustrated by Cecillia Hidayat

NOVELS FOR CHILDREN
The Untameables, by Clare Pollard, illus. by Reena Makwana
Oskar and the Things, by Andrus Kivirähk, illustrated by
Anne Pikkov, translated from Estonian by Adam Cullen

SHORT STORIES AND ESSAYS FOR ADULTS
Bound: A Memoir of Making and Remaking, by Maddie Ballard
How Kyoto Breaks Your Heart, by Florentyna Leow
Tiny Moons: A Year of Eating in Shanghai, by Nina Mingya Powles

Aardvark Day

Victoria Gatehouse

Illustrated by Kate Lucy Foster

THE EMMA PRESS

For my parents

THE EMMA PRESS

First published in the UK in 2026 by The Emma Press Ltd.

Poems © Victoria Gatehouse 2026.
Illustrations © Kate Lucy Foster 2026.

All rights reserved.

The right of Victoria Gatehouse and Kate Lucy Foster to be identified as the creators of this work has been asserted in accordance with the Copyright, Designs and Patents Act 1988.

ISBN 978-1-915628-57-2

A CIP catalogue record of this book is available from the British Library.

Printed and bound by CMP Digital Print Solutions, Poole.
Edited and typeset by Emma Dai'an Wright.

EU GPSR Authorised Representative
LOGOS EUROPE, 9 rue Nicolas Poussin,
17000, LA ROCHELLE, France
E-mail: Contact@logoseurope.eu

The Emma Press
theemmapress.com
hello@theemmapress.com
Jewellery Quarter,
Birmingham, UK

CONTENTS

Poem for a Pebble

I found you on a sad day.

You lay on the pavement's edge
as if someone had kicked you aside,

small, grey and imperfectly round.
Eyes to the ground, I walked past,

then a glint of sun, and you winked
and I *knew* that wink was for me.

You were a perfect fit for my palm
and, close up, so much more than just grey,

with starry sprinkles of pink and cream,
smooth and rough, all at the same time.

I thought of the billions of years
it took to make you this way –

the spit of volcanos, the cold toes of glaciers,
the wild-beating heart of the sea.

You are the secret I hold
in the snug darkness of my pocket.

The Tree and Me

This tree is an ancient king
with a sweeping ivy cloak
and antler-branch crown.

This tree is starting to stumble
on knobble-wobble knees.

This tree has knotted fingers
to hold onto the sky
and lichen tufts to fix
its toes to the ground.

This tree has more eyes
than an alien. This tree
is looking at *me*.

This tree is a playground –
a zip line for spiders,
a see saw for slugs,
a woodlouse funhouse,
a centipede slide.

Best of all, this tree has a hollow
that's just right for me,
a *no-one-can-see* place
to dream and to hide,
a space I can borrow
where, curled up in heartwood,
me can be *tree*
(at least for a while).

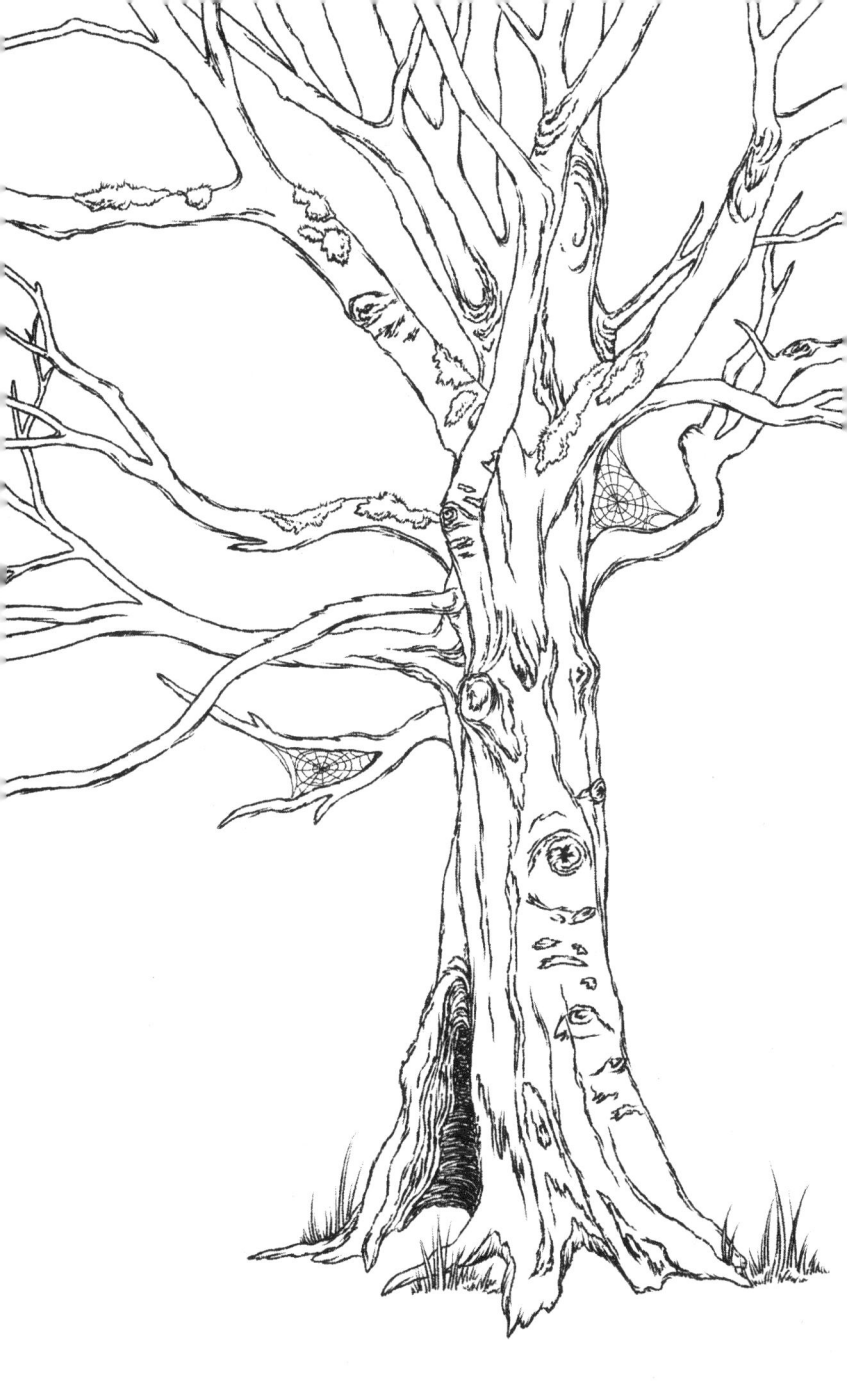

Creaturely Cacophony

the chirping of cheetahs
the clicking of crabs
the barking of piranhas
the roaring of stags
the howling of monkeys
the hooting of chimps
the huffing of pandas
the snapping of shrimp
the growling of seahorses
the hissing of rats
the purring of otters
the squawking of bats

the squeaking of squirrels
the rattling of wrens
the crying of lyrebirds
the cackling of hens
the honking of penguins
the crooning of frogs
the whistling of dolphins
the yipping of dogs
the bellowing of bison
the mewling of cats
the grunting of capybaras
the humming of giraffes

Note: All creatures listed do,
really truly, make these sounds!

Fairy Armadillo

Much as I'd like to keep you
under my pillow,
there are no ants,
no roots or snails
to crunch and nibble.

And though your tummy is fluffy
and you look like a dainty ballerina,
you have serious claws,
a thick, blunt tail,
all your softness encased
in armoured scales.

Fairy armadillo, you don't belong
under anybody's pillow.

You're a pink torpedo,
tunnelling through my dreams,
safe in the shadows of earth.

Note: Fairy armadillos really are pink with fluffy white tummies. They are timid creatures and like to spend their time underground, where they are safe from predators.

A Rockpool is...

A place to bring your bucket
and dream of seahorses and stars.

A goblet from which a giant
can guzzle barnacle broth.

A mermaid's sly and watery eye
that winks in the sun.

A keeper of secrets and seaweed.

A bowl of hidden ledges
to drag your net and stir up clouds.

A pot of slippery fish
and an angry SPLASH of empty.

A secret well to gaze into
deep, deeper
and wait...

Aardvark Day

Today is an aardvark day,
and aardvarks love the dark.

Today I will stay
all snoozy and snug,
curled up in the deep-quilted
burrow of my duvet.

Today I won't stray
from what's gentle and safe
and shadows will wrap themselves
round me like hugs.

Tomorrow I'll find my way
out of this tunnel
and dance in the sun –
yes, tomorrow's the day
for getting things done.

But today is an aardvark day.
and aardvarks *love* the dark.

Beluga Song

They chirp like canaries,
these moon-pale whales –

with mewls and clicks,
bright icy whistles

and playful squawks.
They have no vocal cords

but still, they croak and caw
and squeak and trill as air passes

through special sacs
near their blowholes.

O melon-headed whales
with the gentlest of smiles,

your song is the great
creaking heart of the ocean.

Note: Beluga whales are known for the interesting range of sounds they make, both to communicate and for echolocation. The 'melon' on their heads changes shape as they sing and calves learn to communicate by mimicking their mothers.

Octopus Skin

She disappears at the first sign of trouble,
wraps herself in a cloak of ink.

In the blink of an eye, she can change
from coral-reef *zing*
to blend-into-the-seafloor beige.

But when she sleeps,
her kaleidoscope skin
shape-shifts as she dreams
and a *whoosh* of colour
floods in –

shimmering metallic rainbows,
a cheeky crimson flush.

Note: Octopuses are able to change the colour of their skin so they can blend into the background to keep themselves safe. They can also dazzle by turning their skin into metallic rainbow colours!

How to Be a Dragonfly

Curl into the snug of your egg.

Your body's all wobble and squish,
your skin too tight and eek –
you are split... ting! Relax,
you'll grow into yourself again.

Now it's time to s-t-r-e-t-c-h,
to wriggle your way out and hatch:
a six-legged nymph with a jaw
like a hinge and WHOOSH –

you're breathing out of your bottom,
jet-propelled and ready to go!
Make yourself at home, burrow
into the mud-gloop of pond.

Use your pincers to snatch
a passing tadpole. Gulp it down. Yum!
There are tiny buds on your back
in the place where wings are beginning.

You'll know when to crawl
from those murky depths, let
that old wetsuit *CRACK*,
shed it all and whirr ahead
                              sideways

backwards

then *zoom* as fast as a horse can run.
Just think how far you have come.

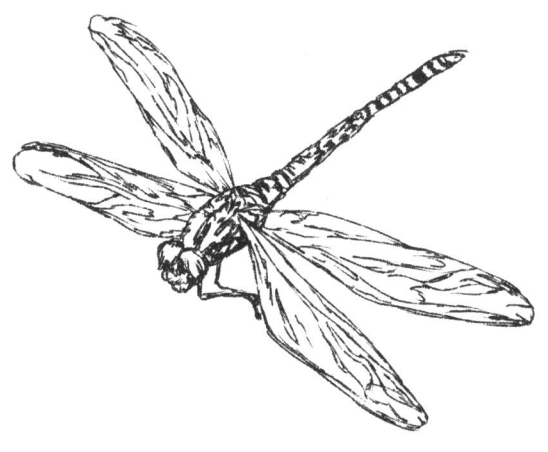

Sloth on Sports Day

It's true, I'm not as speedy as Cheetah:
my sprint is more like a saunter
and my pace in the mid-distance race
is the most dawdling crawl of all.

In fact, a single lap around the track
could take all week, while Tortoise and Snail
whizz past, so fast. Let's face it,
I'll *never* get a spot on the relay team.

Okay, so I may be stupendously slow
but my super-long-super-strong arms
are fantastic at *never* letting go.
When it comes to the gymnast rings
I can hold on
     and on

               and on
          and on…

Dog _vs_ Cat

Dog	Cat
Tail-wagger	Tail-swisher
Sofa-bagger	Spider-squisher
Slipper-taker	Lap-napper
Fur-shaker	Mouse-trapper
Bone-cruncher	Tummy-kneader
Nick-your-luncher	Fussy-feeder
Stick-returner	Alley-stalker
Trick-learner	Fence-top-walker
Sausage-snatcher	Night-prowler
Frisbee-catcher	Moonlight-yowler
Toy-squeaker	All-day-snoozer
Attention-seeker	Pick-n-chooser
Cat-befuddler	Dog-troubler

Fireside-cuddlers

The Butterfly Leaves

Under the eaves
of Nana's shed,
there's a raggedy row
of old brown leaves.

When I ask shall we sweep
them away with the broom,
Nana says leaves can be
butterflies in disguise.

Butterflies with wings
folded up by their sides.
Butterflies sleeping
from winter to spring.

Just imagine the bright splashes
and markings they hide!
A bit like the quietest
boy in our class

thinking no-one was looking
when he opened his book –
only I caught a glimpse
of the beautiful doodles inside.

The Footprints of Elephants

An elephant lifts
her heavy foot
to leave a dent
on dusty ground

and when it rains
the footprint fills
to make the frogs
a micro-pond.

And if the elephant
brings her friends
their tracks combine
to make a trench

where dragonflies
lay eggs and soon
quick-swimming nymphs
will dart and zoom.

The elephants march
munch-crunching scrub
and trimming trees –
clearing paths

so tall giraffes,
graceful gazelles,
and wildebeests
can graze in peace.

And as they walk,
they poop out seeds
which sprout in dung
and shoot out leaves.

These giant beasts,
so slow and kind –
new life is what
they leave behind!

Planet Earth in Reverse

we've left it too late for our planet
nothing you say will persuade me that
the lungs of the Earth could stop wheezing and
endangered creatures might thrive
and if we all worked together
it really *would* make a difference
to switch off standby switches
to build hotels for bugs and bees
to walk or skip or scoot to school
to plant new hedgerows and trees
to turn off dripping taps
it would be a waste of our time
these things are too small to matter and

please don't insist that
we can buy less
we can recycle more
we can avoid single-use plastic
to help reverse the damage
you *must* believe me when I say
children's voices won't be heard
it's just an impossible dream and
don't *ever* imagine that
the trees and the seas will breathe easy
our planet can recover its green

Note: What happens if you read this poem from the bottom to the top? Turn to the next page to see!

Planet Earth In Reverse (mirror poem)

our planet can recover its green
the trees and the seas will breathe easy
don't *ever* imagine that
it's just an impossible dream and
children's voices won't be heard
you *must* believe me when I say
to help reverse the damage
we can avoid single-use plastic
we can recycle more
we can buy less
please don't insist that
these things are too small to matter and
it would be a waste of time
to turn off dripping taps

to plant new hedgerows and trees
to walk or skip or scoot to school
to build hotels for bugs and bees
to switch off standby switches
it really *would* make a difference
and if we all worked together
endangered creatures might thrive
the lungs of the Earth could stop wheezing and
nothing you say will persuade me that
we've left it too late for our planet

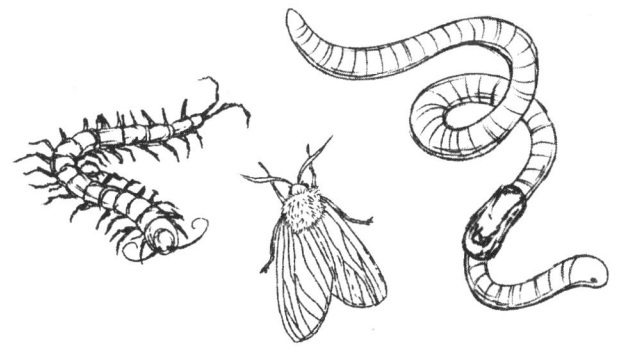

My Litter-Picker

Empty cans, elastic bands, and silver foil aglitter.
With my litter-picker, I pick up all the litter.

Tangled strings and tin-can rings could trap a little critter.
With my litter-picker, I pick up all the litter.

Bottle tops and sodden socks; I really am no quitter!
With my litter-picker, I pick up all the litter.

I take my nan and Matti's mam; I call my baby-sitter.
With our litter-pickers, we pick up all the litter.

Plastic bags are up for grabs; each day we're getting fitter.
With our litter-pickers, we pick up all the litter.

Here's my shout, a BIG call out to all you litter-tippers.
Come bring your litter-pickers. Let's pick up ALL this litter!

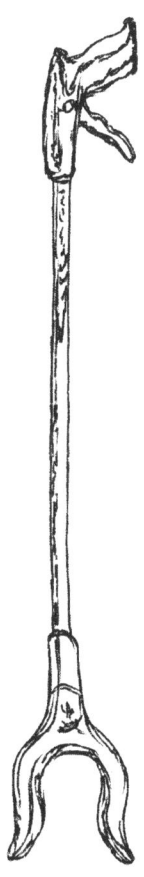

A Weed in Need

A weed needs time to put down roots.
A weed needs soil to send out shoots.
A weed needs lots of rain to drink.
A weed grows faster than you think.

A weed needs sun upon its face.
A weed needs just a little space:
a quiet corner of its own
that isn't sprayed or strimmed or mown.

Who needs the weeds? The butterflies
that flutter-dance across the skies –
the birds, the moths, the beetles too.
Come blow the seeds. This weed needs YOU!

Note: Plants such as dandelions, foxgloves and clover
– all known as weeds – play an important role in
pollination, as well as being bright and beautiful.

Interview with a
Leaf Sheep Sea Slug

So, tell me: are you a leaf?

My body is covered with bright cerata
that wiggle like leaves in the breeze
and, just like a leaf, I need sunlight to feed.

But you are also a… sheep?

I have the face of a cartoon sheep
with black dotty eyes and rhinophore horns
and, just like a sheep, I love to graze on green.

How can you be both leaf AND sheep?

I'm not really either.
I'm a multicoloured slug
who crawls the seafloor and guzzles fuzzy algae.

Does that make you an animal or a plant?

I'm an animal, but…

I can photosynthesise like a plant.

Are you a boy or a girl?

I am both.

Can you sum yourself up in a few lines?

A solar-powered sea-slug,
no bigger than a grain of rice,
with a cheeky sheepy face
and a body of breathing leaves,
an animal who can live as a plant
both female and male
and… wait for it…
I glow in the dark!

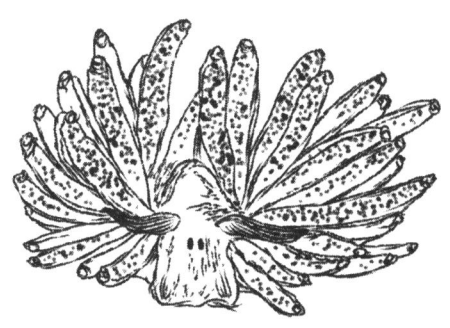

Baby Rays

You might be amazed
to learn that baby stingrays
are like tiny purple aliens
with smiles and whippy tails
dancing round inside
ravioli.

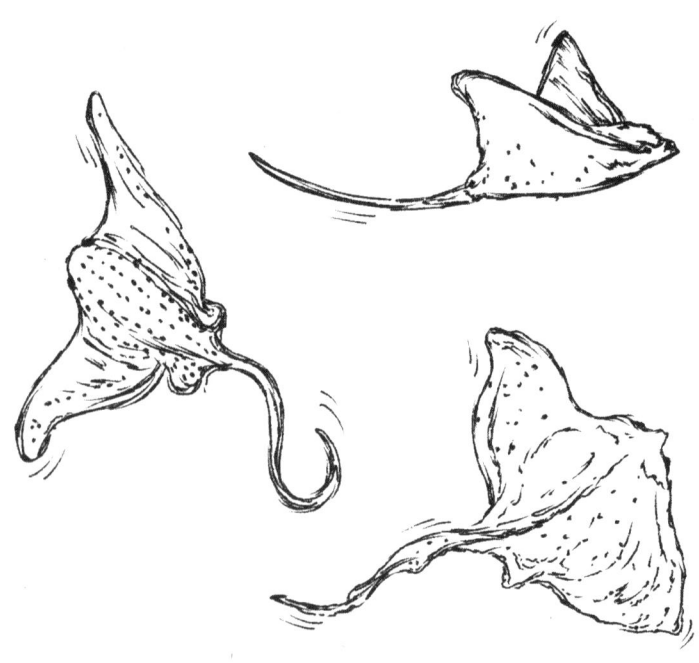

Jelly Alarm!

Should you ever journey
to the ocean's midnight zone
I advise you *not* to nibble
on a passing Atolla jellyfish
(even if you missed your lunch)
as to gobble on their wobble will set off…
FLASHING BLUE LIGHTS!
JELLY ALARM! JELLY ALARM!

And don't even *think* about pulling
their extra-long tentacle,
as a tweak will make them freak and set off…
FLASHING BLUE LIGHTS!
JELLY ALARM! JELLY ALARM!

Leave Atolla jellies alone!
They don't want to be nibbled
or tweaked or grabbed or thrown
and if they even *suspect*
you are trying to do them harm…

FLASHING BLUE LIGHTS!
JELLY ALARM! JELLY ALARM!

Note: Atolla jellyfish really do emit bright blue flashing lights when they feel threatened. They are known as 'alarm jellies'.

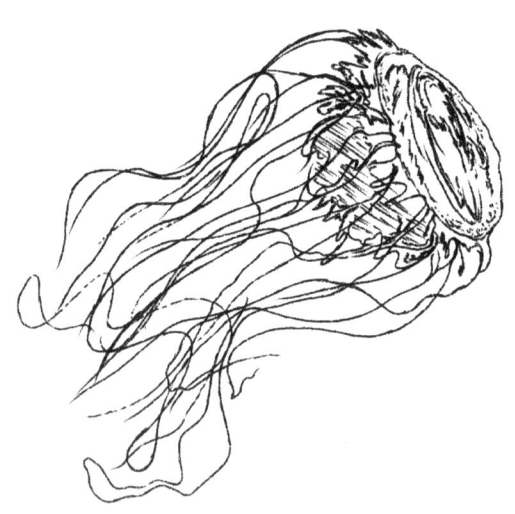

The Smallest Bird in the World

A busy nectar-swigger, that's me!
I flap my wings eighty times a second,
in a blur of whirring, like a hum-thrum bee.

A whizzy sugar-hunter, that's me!
With my super-long tongue I slurp and sip
from nearly two thousand flowers a day.

A razzle-dazzle flyer, that's me!
An acrobat in a vivid green cap,
spreading pollen as I swivel and hover.

A bee hummingbird, that's me!
My eggs are snug as little peas,
tucked in a nest of spider-silk and moss.

White Egret and Black Rhino

Have you heard
of the little white bird
that likes to perch
on the massive grey back
of Black Rhino?

It picks off
the tickly ticks
and bitey mites
because, for this bird,
ticks are delish
and mites a tasty delight.

Black Rhino, then, finally
freed from its itch,
mud-wallows in hollows
while White Egret lingers
on its back until –

CROAK! A warning
if a poacher draws near,
at which point White Egret
and Black Rhino
disappear.

Note: White egrets and black rhinos have a relationship known as symbiotic mutualism. This means that both species benefit from the interaction – which should be the case in all good friendships! Another example in nature is zebras and ostriches. Ostriches have very poor eyesight but a keen sense of smell whereas zebras have great eyesight but a terrible sense of smell. Working together they can protect each other from predators. Bees and flowers are another wonderful example, as bees pollinate flowers and flowers feed the bees.

Poem for a Tear-Drinking Moth

When I'm lying in the dark
with a sob in my throat
I picture the black-chinned antbird
dreaming on a branch in Brazil
while a moth sips salty tears
from the antbird's cheek
so gently that the bird doesn't wake
and I think maybe this moth
might flutter by while I sleep
and drink away *my* tears too –
I promise I won't peek
as the moth sweeps softly in
on shining silver wings.

Truly Strange Mushroom Names

Turkey Tails and Shaggy Manes
Dead Man's Fingers, Vampire's Bane
Lion Shields and Polypores
Puffballs with exploding spores
Frilly orange Chanterelles
Golden Navels, Funeral Bells
Stinkhorns with their whiff of feet
Fly Agarics (do not eat!)
Veiled Ladies, Slippery Jacks
Hairy Brackets, Piggybacks

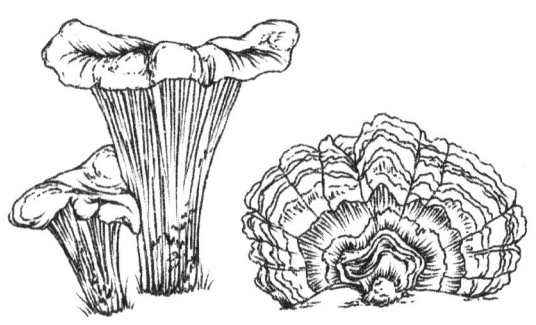

Destroying Angels, ghostly white
Ping-Pong Bats that glow all night
Sprouting Cabbage Parachutes
Wrinkled Peach and Bleeding Tooth
Dainty Dewdrop Dapperlings
Turquoise Elf Cups, Fairy Rings
Morels (eek, they look like brains)
True, but strange, these mushroom names!

I Have a Liking for Lichen Because...

Lichen gives outrageous orange beards
to the craggy faces of rocks.

It can turn a leaf into a mini universe
of splatter-paint stars.

Crispy patches on tree-trunks remind me
of scabs on the kneecaps of giants.

How else would birds find such fabulous frills
to decorate their nests?

Even though I don't want it in my lunchbox,
reindeer absolutely do.

Nothing can brighten a drystone wall
like a lovely green crust of lichen.

Bee Purple

An ultraviolet triolet!

Each flower has a halo, bright,
a colour only bees can see
with special super-hero sight.
Each flower has a halo, bright,
a nectar-glow of purple light,
a gleam beyond our frequency.
Each flower has a halo, bright,
a colour only bees can see.

Note: Bee Purple is a mix of ultraviolet
and yellow light, not visible to humans.
Bees love this colour, which attracts them
to nectar-rich plants.

Bamboo Stew

Let's eat bamboo
like pandas do –
such fun to munch
our bamboo brunch!

Bamboo on toast,
a bamboo roast,
a bamboo stew,
bamboo fondue,

bamboo-shoot cake
with bamboo shake,
then dunk your chips
in bamboo dips.

Come join our crew –
we'll chew, chew, chew
all this bamboo
like pandas do!

Poem for Peat

I want to sink into
wetlands and fens,
to be swamped by the swamplands
and bogged down by bogs,
squishy, delicious
and packed with peat
in peppy layers of magic
like the best chocolate cake.

Peat has so much to teach us:
that we can take things   slow;
one millimetre a year is progress;
if we wait, things will grow –

tufts of cotton-grass,
feathery bogbean stars,
insect-eating sundews,
their tentacles oozing glue...

Peat keeps rare creatures
in the folds of its cloak –
curve-bill curlews,
zig-zag adders,
nibble-nose
    water voles,
emperor moths
with spotted wings
and copper-eyed toads.

It takes thousands of years to make a bog
and long may the peatlands remain –
brimming with wildlife
luminous with moss,
holding a sky-full of rain.

Which Frog Superpower Would You Choose?

Webbed fingers and flappy skin under your
   arms, like a gliding leaf frog.

Flashing crimson headlights to scare people
   away, like a red-eyed tree frog.

Cunningly curved fangs as a tadpole, like a
   vampire flying frog
(black swirling cloak is optional).

To turn see-through while you sleep, like a
   glass frog.

To dazzle like a sapphire, with brilliant skin
   like a blue poison frog
(note: you are *way* too toxic to be hugged).

To make a wheezy-squeezy-car-honking
   noise like a green tree frog
   (or to woof like a barking tree frog).

To chill in a bubble on a leaf, like the
   grey foam-nest tree frog (forget about
   superpowers!).

A Lizard Has Two Modes

1. Lightning Mode

I run   on sun
        kick-started
            by sparks
see me zap
            and zip   and zing
on the bling
    of the light
see how fast   I can dash
    flashing past   *all pizzazz*
see the pep
    in my step   how quick
I nip
    in a tail's   whippy flick
        from wall
        to leaf
to twig
all verve   all vim   such fun
that is   until

I run   out   of   sun...

(skip to Lounge Mode)

2. Lounge Mode

My blood has turned cold
I'm stuck in the rut of go-slow
my gusto is spluttering on zero
I must wait for a bright new day
for a toasty rock or sun-baked stone
a place of my own to loll
and laze in the haze of the rays
where my skin will grow dark
to soak up more light
'cos I'm a laid-back sun-lounger
an idle heat-scrounger
the sun's smiley glow will
give me back my get up and go
I'll be fizzy
        all whizzy
                absolutely
re-booted and ready to
        scoot...

(return to Lightning Mode)

Hope is a Hedgerow

Together we're planting a hedgerow
of hawthorn
    and hazel
      and dog rose.
A hideout of holly and briar.
A fortress where birds can nest.
A soil perfector. A flood protector.
A field-connector. A butterfly collector.
A stronghold for toads.
A pipistrelle pit-stop.
A dormouse corridor.
A hedgehog highway. A bumble-bee flyway.

Our hedgerow will grow as we grow.
Today, we'll take skinny saplings
of hazel

      and hawthorn

              and dog rose
and plant an absolute belter of a shelter
to help the small creatures of tomorrow.

Advice from the Minibeasts

Learn to glide in the rain says Slug.
Put a waggle in your dance says Bee.
And a wriggle in the soil says Worm.

Woodlouse says *Roll up, roll up –*
it's okay to stay under your rock.

When you work as a team says Ant,
you can carry much more than you think.

Millipede says *Don't waste all day*
counting your own legs.

If your web breaks says Spider,
you can spin another one, better.

Caterpillar says *Your wings are there –*
you just haven't found them yet.

If someone annoys you Ladybird says,
just wee on them.

Switch on your lights says Firefly –
we all have our own way of glowing.

You'll get there in the end says Snail,
in your own slime…

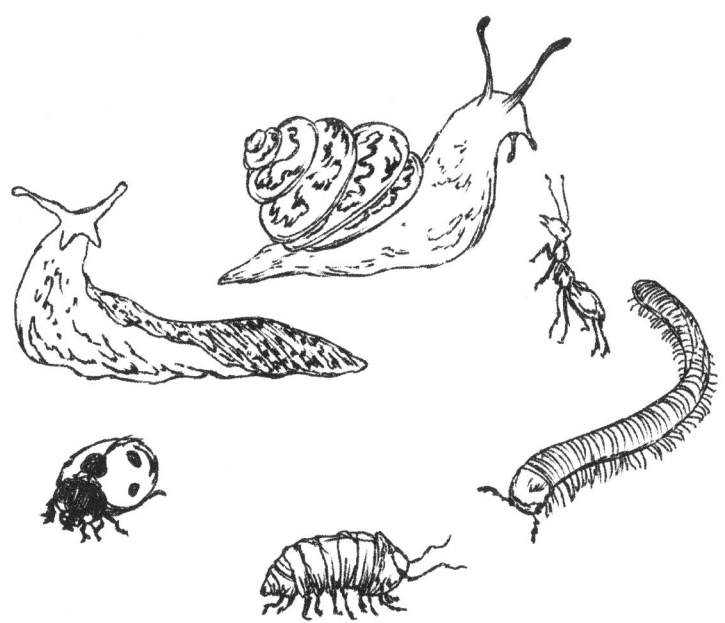

Otter Pockets

I love the way sea otters
float on their backs,
while gently holding
each other's paws.

But that's not
my favourite thing
about them.

What I like most
is that little flap of skin,
in the tickle
of their armpit –

a safe and secret pocket
to stash a shellfish snack
and sometimes to keep
a special pebble in.

BONUS BITS!

INTERVIEW WITH AUTHOR
VICKY GATEHOUSE

When did you start writing poems?

I loved making up poems and rhymes in my head from a very young age. I think I was about 8 years old when I began to write them down.

Do you remember the first poem you wrote?

Yes! It was called 'The Haunted House'. I remember sitting at the kitchen table, experimenting with rhyme and spooky vocabulary. The poem featured bats, witches' cats, cobwebs and the eerie hooting of an owl. It was very dramatic poem and a lot of fun to write. I can still recite some of the lines even now!

What was your favourite subject at school?

I looked forward to story time as a young child, when the teacher would read aloud to the class. As I grew older, I became passionate about creative writing, science and anything which involved doing my own research. There was a public library next door to my school and sometimes we were allowed to choose a book and have some quiet reading time – this was always a treat (Dr Seuss books in particular)!

How did you become a zoologist?

Well, at university, I started off studying chemistry. After a year I realised I wasn't enjoying it as much as I'd hoped. Luckily, I got the chance to attend some zoology lectures and absolutely loved them. My tutors kindly allowed me to change courses, so I ended up taking zoology with biochemistry (the chemistry of humans, plants and animals – fascinating stuff!). I went on to do project work in marine biology and still have a special interest in ocean creatures.

Which frog superpower would you choose?

All of them! Seriously, if I had to choose just one it would be to have flappy wing-like skin so I could leap around the treetops like a gliding leaf frog!

Which is your favourite illustration in the book?

This is *such* a difficult question because all Kate's

illustrations are amazing. I admire her attention to detail and the way each creature (and plant) has its own personality on the page. If I had to choose, it would be the gorgeous otters in the final poem, each holding a special stone. It was also a thrill to see the cover for the first time. The aardvark's nightcap is wonderfully quirky!

And finally, what advice would you give to young writers?

Don't be afraid of an empty page – there's no right or wrong way to start a piece of writing. Take a deep breath, then let your imagination soar and your pencil flow. Be as messy and experimental as you like – you can always take words out, or add them in, later. Remember, your imagination (and your own way of experiencing the world) are unique to you and will make your writing special.

I would also say read, read and read some more! Delving into books and poems by other people can inspire you to write your own...

WRITE YOUR OWN POEMS!

To get you started, here are some ideas from editor Emma Dai'an Wright:

✳ Are there any trees near you? Maybe one you can see from your window, or one you walk past quite often? Vicky has a poem about a favourite tree on page 3, where she describes it a bit like a person, with fingers and eyes. Write a poem about a tree that you know.

If you can, go and look at the tree up close, and note down as much about it as possible: its shape, its texture, what insects and animals seem to like it too. If it's not wintertime, what are its leaves like? Put all your observations into your poem. To help you structure your poem, you can try starting every line with 'This tree'.

✳ Aardvarks have the right idea! The poem on page 11 tells us about a snuggly day, taking inspiration from how aardvarks live. Write a poem about your ideal cosy day. Imagine you have nowhere to be and nothing you need to

do. Where will you spend your day? What/who will you have around you? Will there be snacks?

✳ In 'Beluga Song' on page 14, we learn about the sounds these whales make, both to help find their way around (echolocation) and to communicate with each other. Imagine you understand the sounds of beluga whales and you're listening in to a group of them (a pod!). Write down some ideas about what you might overhear, and write a poem about what the whales are saying.

✳ Vicky gives dogs and cats lots of new names on page 22: 'Nick-your-luncher' and 'Fussy-feeder' are some of my favourites! Pick an animal (like a badger) and make a list of all the things it does. You might need to read more about it, to help add to your list – or you could choose a pet and make a list of what this specific animal does. Then make these actions into a poem: it could just be a poem about the animal, or you could do it in the style of 'Dog vs Cat' and make those actions into names.

✳ On page 36 we have an interview with a very unusual-looking animal: the leaf sheep sea slug. Is there any animal you would like to have a chat with? Imagine a conversation with that animal – what would you ask it? What might it reply? Would it ask you anything too? You can look up some facts about the animal for this poem, or you can just make it up from your imagination – this is your interview and your poem!

✳ We might not always like it, but there are usually insects inside our home. The speaker in 'Poem for a Tear-Drinking Moth' on page 44 does like the idea of it, and finds getting a visit from the moth quite comforting. I am not a fan of the tiny flies that came in with the apples this winter, but I can see they have made themselves at home in my kitchen, especially round the tap. Think of the insects you have seen in your home (flies? bees? beetles? ants?), pick one, and write a poem from its point of view. How did it get in? Where does it live? What does it think of your home? What does it think of you?

ACKNOWLEDGEMENTS

I am grateful to the editors of the following magazines and anthologies where poems from this book (or versions of them) have appeared: *Little Thoughts Press* 'Gold Wild' edition, *Northern Gravy*, *Spelt*, *Tyger Tyger*, and *You're Never too Much: Poems for Every Emotion* (Pan Macmillan).

Thank you, Kate, for bringing the creatures and plants in these poems to life in the most wonderful way. You're an incredible illustrator and I'm lucky to work with you!

Sincere gratitude to Rachel Piercey and the amazingly talented 'Zigzaggers' who have taught me so much and generously supported my children's writing journey.

Finally, a massive thank you to Emma, Georgia, James, Ella and everyone at The Emma Press for being a joy to collaborate with and for making my dreams come true by publishing this book.

ABOUT THE AUTHOR

Vicky Gatehouse is an award-winning poet and children's writer, based in Yorkshire. She originally trained as a zoologist and loves to write about animals and nature. Vicky's poems for children have appeared in *Tyger Tyger*, *The Toy*, *Little Thoughts Press*, *Northern Gravy*, and various Pan Macmillan anthologies. She was Highly Commended for the Caterpillar Prize, 2025.

Vicky's poetry for adults is widely published and she has won, or been placed in, many competitions, including the Ginkgo Prize for Ecopoetry in 2023. A pamphlet of Vicky's poetry for adults, *The Mechanics of Love*, published by Smith | Doorstop, was selected as a 'Laureate's Choice' by Carol Ann Duffy in 2019, and her debut adult's collection, *The Hawthorn Bride* was published by Indigo Dreams in 2024.

ABOUT THE ILLUSTRATOR

 Kate Lucy Foster creates illustrations that are 'natural, cosy and textural'. She is inspired by the world around her and loves to incorporate nature into her work. She combines traditional printmaking, sketching, painting and digital work to give her illustrations an authentic, hand-made quality. Kate studied illustration at Birmingham City University.

WEBSITE: www.katefoster.co.uk

INSTAGRAM: @katefoster_art

ABOUT THE EMMA PRESS

The Emma Press is an independent publishing house based in Birmingham. It was founded in 2012 by Emma Dai'an Wright and has grown to five part-time staff members following support from Arts Council England's Elevate programme in 2020-23.

The Emma Press specialises in poetry, short fiction and children's books, with translations across all genres. Recent publications have won the Michael Marks Illustration Award and been shortlisted for the CLiPPA and the Week Junior Book Awards.

In 2024 the Emma Press was a Regional Finalist for Small Press of the Year Award in the British Book Awards, as well as shortlisted for the Independent Publishers Guild's Alison Morrison Diversity, Equity & Inclusion Award.

theemmapress.com
@TheEmmaPress